BROTHER FRANCIS
The Life of
Francis of Assisi

BROTHER FRANCIS
The Life of Francis of Assisi

by
JAKOB STREIT

Silhouette Illustrations by Roland Marti

Translated from German by Nina Kuettel

Printed with support from the Waldorf Curriculum Fund

Published by:
Waldorf Publications
Research Institute for Waldorf Education
38 Main Street
Chatham, NY 12037

Title: *Brother Francis: The Life of Francis of Assisi*
Author: Jakob Streit
Translator: Nina Kuettel
Illustrator: Roland Marti
German title: *Bruder Franz: Das Leben des Francesco von Assisi*
Publisher: Urachhaus, 1997
ISBN # 3-8251-7077-2
Proofreader, Layout: Ann Erwin

© 2013 by AWSNA
Reprinted 2014 by Waldorf Publications

ISBN # 978-1-936367-40-5

Contents

The Lute Player 7

Then He Met His Gaze 11

In Prison 14

The Raid 15

The Transformation 16

The Encounter 18

He Leaves His Father's House 20

The Beggar of San Damiano 23

The Brothers of Portiuncula 25

The Oxen Brother 26

Angelo and the Thieves 28

Clara and Her Sisters 32

The Fierce Wolf 34

The Cricket in the Fig Tree 36

The Bird Sermon 37

Brother Donkey 39

The Grotto Christmas 40

On Mount Alverno 41

The Canticle of the Sun 45

The Peacemaker 50

Farewell to Earthly Life 52

The Lute Player

There was once a fun-loving, handsome lad named Francis. One evening he was playing the lute high up on the roof terrace when night began to fall. In the little town of Assisi where he lived, Italian was spoken, but Francis was singing a French song. His mother was from France and she had taught him to sing. He was trying to pick out the melody, so he was singing very quietly until everything sounded in harmony.

The Moon had just come up. Francis paused his playing and looked with awe at the silver disc in the sky. Suddenly, it seemed as if the Moon had a face and it winked at him. He plucked a few more notes, looked up at the Moon, and this time it seemed to be smiling at him. Francis laughed back at the Moon and said: "I will sing to you!" In a full voice, he began to sing his cheerful, French song so that it resounded far over the rooftops of the little town.

Soon a few boys gathered in the square in front of the house. They were very well acquainted with their friend up there. They would have liked to join him, but they knew his wealthy father was a strict, aristocratic gentleman. He would never allow boys from the street inside his house. But they wanted to give the singer on the roof a sign of friendship. They quickly gathered up a few small rocks. One of the boys took them in his cupped hand and, with good aim, flung them up to the terrace so that Francis was mute with surprise. He stood up, looked over the railing down to the square, and recognized his friends' shadows.

One of them called up: "Francis, come down! We want to sing with you!"

The singer thought for a moment, then replied: "Vengo, I'm coming!" Since his father was away on business for a few days, Francis thought: 'I'll bring my friends up here. Mother is sound asleep in her room.'

The boys silently climbed the stairs in their soft-soled shoes. Some sat and some reclined on the stone floor and listened to Francis's joyful singing and playing. Suddenly, one of them saw a black cat slinking along the roof in the moonlight, tail held aloft, meowing loudly. Francis immediately switched to a song about cats, this time in Italian. At the end of each verse there was a string of "meows" and the boys all meowed along.

One of them shouted: "Francis, sing us a donkey song so we can hee-haw!" The singer immediately began to sing the praises of Brother Donkey, who worked long hours and sometimes was given the whip. When the hee-haw chorus came around, they all neighed and whinnied along.

The noise from the rooftop terrace grew louder and louder. Downstairs, inside the house, Mother woke up. She threw on a robe and climbed the stairs to the terrace. Secretly she peeked through the crack in the door at the group of singers and smiled. Everything that Francis, her only son and darling, did was all right with her. And she knew that singing chased away evil thoughts. But it was good that his father, Bernardone, was not here. She tiptoed back to her room and fell back asleep.

Suddenly Francis stopped playing. He slapped one of his friends on the shoulder and said: "Come with me. We're going to go get something!" In the cellar, Francis felt his way to two jugs of wine. The boys carried them carefully back to the terrace. Now something was going on! Singing was thirsty work. Soon it was much louder with hooting laughter.

When the jugs were empty one of them said: "Let's go through the town and wake up the sleeping people!" No sooner said than done. They rumbled down the stairs to the cobblestone lane, a singing Francis in the lead with all the boys meowing, neighing and hee-hawing behind. So they went throughout the moon-bright village. Some people were angry and screamed out their windows, but others thought the singing was fun, and they just turned over and went back to sleep.

The night watchman stepped into their path with a lantern and spear. He said: "Quiet, quiet, gentleman. Let the citizens have their sleep!" Francis immediately came up with a song:

> Quiet, quiet, gentlemen.
> Let the citizens have their sleep!
> But the tomcats chase mice – meow,
> Chase mice – meow – meow,
> And the donkeys have fleas – and how!
> Hee-haw, hee-haw, hee-haw...

Soon the boys were singing along. The sound carried up and down the lanes, and the night watchman limped along behind them until the bell struck one. He happily stuck Francis's coin into his pocket, and the boys all went home.

From then on more and more young men started hanging around Francis, and they all had a great time in the village taverns.

Then He Met His Gaze

Francis's father, Bernardone, owned a luxury fabric store. The place practically glowed from the silks and velvets and the gold and silver threads woven into them. The wealthy ladies of the town and the surrounding castle estates liked to shop at Bernardone's.

Francis's father said to him: "You may help your mother with sales in the shop. You should concentrate on serving the young noble ladies. They pay a good price for everything that catches their fancy!"

One day Francis was helping some aristocratic customers. He rolled out the precious fabric for the women. Just then a ragged, old beggar walked into the shop, stretched a trembling hand toward Francis, and whispered: "For the sake of Christ!"

Irritated at the interruption, Francis pointed him to the door. Then he met the old man's gaze, eye to eye, and he saw the whole misery of the man's life staring back at him. The beggar shyly retreated and disappeared.

Francis accepted the coins from the knight who accompanied the ladies and threw them into the money box. As he was closing it and turning the key, he sunk his head for a moment and once again saw the mournful eyes of the beggar in his mind's eye.

He went to the door, hurried out, and wandered around town searching. Where did he go?

Finally he found the elderly man at a water seller's stand who was just pouring some water into his cupped hands. Francis saw how the elderly one drank thirstily. He thought: 'The poor water seller gave him to drink. But I gruffly showed him the door, even as he bid me in Christ's name.'

Francis walked up to the beggar, shook the contents of his money purse into the man's hand, and some of the silver coins even fell to the ground. Before the old beggar could begin to thank him, Francis was gone. With this gift, the man was able to secure his living for a long time.

In Prison

The town of Assisi and the town of Perugia had become enemies. Francis and his friends armed themselves in order to take part in a sneak attack on Perugia. But the Perugians were watchful and many of the youthful warriors from Assisi were taken prisoner and brought to the town jail. Sparse food and the horrible boredom left the youths crippled with despair.

Only one of them did not let imprisonment get him down: Francis. He talked to his comrades: "One day we will be free again. We are young. Our lives are before us. We will carry arms again and maybe become famous for heroic acts. Who wouldn't want to be knighted?!" Then he sang them a song of hope, of love, of happiness; he told them made-up adventure stories and jokes. Their imprisonment lasted almost an entire year. There were hours – even days – when Francis himself despaired: 'What will become of my life?'

When peace was finally declared between Assisi and Perugia, Francis and his fellow prisoners were freed. Now he knew: 'I want to go out into the world! I want to become a fighter and a knight, and earn honor and fame.'

The Raid

Francis's father, Bernardo, agreed with his son's desire to become a noble knight. Francis was able to buy shining weapons and a thoroughbred horse. His clothing and armor were equal to any knight. So he left his home to take part in a raid in southern Italy.

Along the way something strange happened. One night Francis had a prophetic dream. In it, someone called him by name and led him into a spacious, splendid palace. There were many weapons stored in an armory. Superb shields and iron weapons of every kind hung on the walls, promising glory and fame. Francis asked enthusiastically: "Who owns this palace?"

A voice answered: "It will belong to you!"

When Francis awoke from his dream, he thought: 'I must be on the right path – on my way to worldly glory, glamor and riches.'

A little while later, Francis had the same dream again. As he was standing in the armory, the voice said: "Francis, try to understand the dream in another way. You should not acquire earthly weapons, but rather spiritual weapons. You should fight for good in the world and against evil. Return home and you will be told what to do."

When Francis awoke from this dream, and caught a glimpse of his sword, his shield and his spear, they seemed foreign to him. The same day he gave away all his armor to a poor nobleman and started the journey home to Assisi, deep in thought about everything he had experienced.

The Transformation

After his return home to Assisi, Francis came down with a bad fever that brought him to the brink of death. His mother cared for him day and night and often prayed by his bedside. In his delirium of fever, the patient cried out and spoke as if he were fighting with demons. But after many days, a peace came over him and, mercifully, he was able to sleep.

Francis recovered, and when he could once again mingle among his family and friends, he was completely changed. His old friends did not understand why he did not want to go out and celebrate with them. His father was angry because Francis began giving his clothing away to the poor, and was no longer the son he had admired. His father also thought that thieves had taken Francis's armor and that made him very angry.

But in Francis's mind the idea of making a pilgrimage to Rome was taking shape. He hoped that he would receive some direction for his life at the grave of the Apostle Peter.

When Francis arrived in Rome there were many beggars gathered in front of St. Peter's Basilica, waiting for alms. He walked up to one of them, laid a silver coin in his hand, and said: "Please, let me exchange my clothing for yours!" The beggar looked at the elegantly dressed gentleman and thought: 'Is he making fun of me?' But he could see that the young man was genuine. Francis removed his torn mantle, and the stranger exchanged it for his own.

Now Francis was a beggar like all the others. He went to St. Peter's tomb. He left all the rest of his money at the tomb as a sacrifice. He lingered long, sunk in prayer. When he arose, he returned to the place of beggars, and they shared their bread with him.

Cheerful and happy, Francis traveled from Rome back to Assisi. He was not afraid to beg farmers along the way for meager food. When he returned home, his father Bernardo was appalled by his son. He thought, again, that someone had robbed him. But Francis confided in his mother: "You see, my dear mother, I want to be poor just as Christ's disciples were. I want to be like them." Pica, his mother, understood Francis with her heart. When his father argued with him, his mother tried to calm her husband.

The Encounter

During these days Francis often walked or rode aimlessly in the surrounding countryside of Assisi. His father had taken his beggar's robe, ripped it up, tossed it out, and given Francis another respectable one to replace it. One day while he was riding around the area, he came upon an outcast. Because the man had a contagious disease, he was not allowed in the village. He lived on the outskirts, disdained and shunned, simply waiting to die.

As Francis rode up to him, a feeling of deep sympathy for the man's plight overcame him. He dismounted his horse and walked to him whose skin was eaten away by the sickness. Francis hugged him, pressed him to his chest, and said: "Dear, poor Brother!" Then Francis grabbed the man's hand and kissed it. The outcast did not know what was happening. The young stranger gave him a gold coin before he rode away.

The next day Francis took some money with him, purchased bread and fruit, and some wound salve and strips of linen. He rode outside the village where the outcasts were gathered so that he could help them and be of service to them. He washed their wounds, covered them with ointment and bandaged them. Such healing love streamed forth from his hands that many of the sick people slowly got better.

Once, as he was returning home, Francis rode by an old, tumble-down, little church called San Damiano. He stopped suddenly because it was as if a voice was saying: "Go inside!"

Not one candle was burning; no oil lamp lit up the room. In the half-darkness Francis could make out a cross. He knelt before it and prayed to Him who was crucified. A mild, pleasant voice spoke to his soul: "Francis, do you not see how my house has been ruined? Go and restore it!"

Francis answered: "I will gladly do it, my Lord!" Once again, Francis felt the warm light of Christ illuminating his soul. After a little time had passed, Francis walked out of the chapel and saw Father Pietro, sitting on a stone bench. Francis went up to him and said: "My dear Don Pietro, from now on, an oil lamp shall burn before the painting of the Cross inside the chapel. Here, take my money purse to buy new oil! When that money is spent, I will give you more; as much as you need."

Francis left the place with tears running down his cheeks. Again and again, thoughts of the suffering One on the Cross came to his mind. And he knew that he was to begin with the restoration of the little Church of San Damiano.

Francis Leaves His Father's House

Francis needed quarried stones, boards and mortar in order to repair the walls of San Damiano. To have some money for this purpose, he took one of the many bolts of fabric from his father's shop to sell in the neighboring village of Foligno. But the earnings seemed too little, so he sold his horse as well. He returned on foot to San Damiano with a handsome sum. He wanted to give all of his earnings to Father Pietro for the little church. But the priest said: "Francis, what will your father say? It is his money, after all. I cannot accept it."

Francis put the money purse on a window niche and began to clean the floor and walls to prepare them for the renovation. He did not return home, but he lay down in a corner of the church and slept there.

Francis feared that his father would try to bring him home by force. So the next day, he found a remote cave in the cliffs above Assisi. It served as a makeshift resting place. Here, undisturbed, he could observe his long prayer time every day. A discreet servant of his mother, who was loyal to Francis, brought him food once in a while. Even though the cave was very dark, Francis always felt flooded with a wonderful light that warmed his soul.

It was not long before his father discovered his hiding place. Servants helped him drag his son back home. He locked Francis in a dingy cellar for a few days. After all his pleading did not change Francis's intentions, Bernardone struck him very hard and put him in chains. But Francis would not give in. He had become the laughing stock of the town. Francis bore it all in silence, with patience; but he did not change his mind.

After some time had passed, his father had to go away on business. Francis's mother ordered that her tortured son be freed from his chains, and she had a long talk with him. As he opened his heart to her, she realized that Francis needed to be free to go his own way. She let him return alone to his quiet hermit's cave.

When his father returned, his anger blazed also against Francis's mother. He made a complaint against her to the Bishop of Assisi. The Bishop sent a messenger to Francis and invited him for an interview. He was acquainted with the youth and said: "How beautiful it is that you want to serve God! But the money you got from selling the cloth and the horse belongs to your father. Bring it here. It will help to ease your father's anger."

Francis replied: "Sir, not only will I return the money that belongs to him with a cheerful heart, but my clothing also."

At an agreed upon time, the Bishop brought together father and son. Bernardone came with several town councilmen. The Bishop greeted him. Suddenly, Francis stepped out from a room in the house where he had been waiting. In one hand he held the money purse and on the other arm, all of his clothes. He said: "Listen, all you who are gathered here, and understand me well: Up to now I have called Pietro Bernardone my father. Today I give back to him what is his. As I have decided to serve the Highest Lord, from now on I will say: 'Our Father, thou art in Heaven!' "

With these words, Francis laid the money and clothes on the ground. Bernardone paled and remained silent. But the Bishop was moved by the youth's courage and strength of will. He covered the naked man with his own mantle and sent him on his way in a pilgrim's robe. From that moment on, Francis had a good friend in the Bishop.

The Beggar of San Damiano

Towards evening, after leaving the Bishop's palace, Francis came to the little San Damiano Church. An oil lamp illuminated the painting of the Crucifixion, while all around it was darkness. Francis felt a deep sense of happiness. He was now free of all obligations and could live in poverty as the Disciples of Christ had done. The whole night he spent alternating between praying and dreaming and sleeping, and back to praying, alone in the little chapel. Early in the morning, as the birds were greeting the sunrise, Francis started the repairs to the walls while singing songs of praise and gratitude.

In Assisi he begged for the quarry stones that were lying around here and there. In the beginning people laughed at the foolish, young man. But when they saw how intent he was on meeting his goal, and how the little church was looking better and better, many of them began to admire his determination. Yes, there were even some young men with whom he had earlier caroused the night away who were now helping him to carry stones and mix mortar. He taught his friends that is was possible to do even heavy labor with a sense of joy. Those who stayed with him he called "Brother."

For his meals, Francis was not shy about going around to the houses of the village with his bowl and asking for food scraps. He hung a small cup on his belt to gather donations of oil for the church lamp. When he noticed young men hanging around with nothing to do, he would speak to them: "Come with me and help with the renovation of the San Damiano Church!" And so the reconstruction

work progressed very nicely, to the great satisfaction of the church's priest, Father Pietro.

One day, during Mass, Francis heard the priest read this passage from the Gospel of Matthew: "And as ye go, preach, heal the sick, cleanse the lepers, provide neither gold, nor silver, nor brass in your purses, nor scrip for your journey, neither two coats, neither shoes, nor yet staffs."

Francis was jubilant: 'That is how my Brothers and I will live.' And so, he took on a life of poverty and called it his "Sister."

The Brothers of Portiuncula

When Francis happened upon people, he always greeted them with: "The Lord give you peace!" When he said "thank-you" for donations, often he would add a short verse from the Gospels. From these greetings and words of gratitude, slowly he developed short sermons, and his words reached people's hearts rather than only their minds.

The renovations on San Damiano were now finished. But Francis knew of a another project, a chapel below the village called Portiuncula. It stood there, abandoned and barren, in an open field. With three other Brothers he got to work. Next to the chapel, each man built himself a little hut made of brushwood and straw. A fifth man, Sylvester, joined their group. He was actually a priest. Before he came to Francis, he had a powerful dream. In the dream he looked upon a wild dragon that had wound his snake-like body around the whole town of Assisi. Smoke and flames rose up, and it seemed the whole area would go under. Then, Brother Francis ascended over the dragon. A golden cross shone forth from his mouth. It grew and grew. The tip of it touched the sky and the beam spread across the wide Earth. The dragon had to draw back from the brilliant light streaming out of the cross.

For three nights in a row Sylvester had the same dream. Then he was certain: 'I will become Francis's Brother, for he is joined with the Cross of Christ.' Francis was delighted to accept him at Portiuncula.

The Oxen Brother

Francis was in the habit of carrying a whisk broom on his belt in order to clean the churches before he gave a sermon. Once he came to a small church that stood in the middle of a cultivated field. Francis went inside and began to sweep with the little broom.

In the field next to the church, a young farmer named Giovanni was plowing. He recognized Francis, left the two oxen standing, and went inside the church. "Brother," he said to Francis, "Give me the broom! I want to help you." He took the broom and did a good job.

The two of them sat on a church bench to rest, and Giovanni said: "Dear Brother, for a long time I have wanted to serve God, all the more because I have heard such good things about you and your Brothers. But I did not know how I could meet you. I want to be your Brother and do whatever you think best."

Francis put his hand on Giovanni's shoulder and replied: "If you want to share your life among us Brothers, you must bring all your possessions and give them to the poor."

Immediately, Giovanni got up, went to the field and returned to the church with one ox. He said: "This ox is my inheritance. You may give it to the poor, and I will come with you as your Brother!"

Francis had to smile at Giovanni's good intentions. But when Giovanni's parents, who were also in the field, came up with their other children, the situation took a turn. They had observed the strange transaction. Moaning and whining, they pleaded to have the coveted animal returned.

Francis said: "I will give back the ox in exchange for the Brother." That is how Francis came to have his "Oxen Brother." It was said of Giovanni that he copied every movement and gesture that Francis did. Whether he kneeled, cried, or sang, Giovanni did exactly the same, so much did he love his Brother-master.

Angelo and the Thieves

Once Francis was preaching from the fullness of his heart in the marketplace of a small village. A finely dressed young gentleman walked up to him and asked: "Francis, I would like to change my life. May I travel with you and become your Brother?"

Francis replied: "You are from an aristocratic house and still so young. Think about it – poverty travels with us. Could you bear that?"

"Yes! That is what I want! Take me with you!" Francis looked into his pleading eyes. He was happy about the young man and gave him his blessing. Because he possessed aristocratic good looks, he was called Angelo – Angel. He was allowed to build himself a hut in Portiuncula.

At that time three robbers were plaguing Assisi and its surroundings, carrying out very many misdeeds. One day these three showed up at the Brothers' place. Angelo was there by himself. They snarled: "Give us something to eat!"

Angelo recognized the scoundrels and said: "You reprobate no-goods! You have harmed many residents, and now you come to God's servants to steal away our alms? You don't deserve to walk upon the Earth. Get out of here, and don't let me see you again!"

As angry and full of resentment as they were, the robbers still did not dare stand against the youth, who looked like an avenging angel. So they ran away, cursing.

A little while later, Francis returned to the hermitage. He brought the alms he had collected, a sack full of bread and a bottle of wine. Angelo, chin held high, excitedly told how he had chased off the malicious thieves. Francis looked at him for a few moments, silent and serious, and then said: "Angelo, do you believe that your harsh words have helped those lost souls one little bit? Sinners can be brought to their senses through gentleness. Christ said: 'I have not come for the righteous, but for the sinners.' So, I order you now: Take this sack of bread and wine. Hurry after the three and search until you find them. Offer them food and drink in my name. Humbly ask their forgiveness. Tell them I would be happy to see them!"

Angelo hurried. He found the thieves resting under a tree and did exactly as Francis said. While they were eating the bread and passing around the wine bottle, they talked among themselves. Angelo waited a little to the side for the sack and the bottle. The robbers felt as if they were suddenly looking at all their terrible acts. They blamed each other and finally decided they would go together to Brother Francis and ask his advice.

When Francis saw the three thieves nearing his place with Angelo, he out went to greet them. He shook hands with each one and said: "Peace be with you!"

In a muffled voice, the first one said: "Francis, we are bad men. Will you hear our confessions?"

Francis replied: "Yes, I will hear them, if I may tell you also of my own sins." He went with them to the chapel.

After a few hours, when the evening was growing dark, Francis left the three. He went to Angelo's hut and said to him: "Please put an oil lamp and some bread and wine on the altar for them. Tonight they will sleep in the chapel!"

A little while later Angelo quietly crept into the dark room with the lamp. He found the three men sleeping on the floor around the altar. He gently laid the lamp, bread and wine upon it. He made the sign of the cross over each sleeping figure and murmured a blessing before quietly closing the door behind him.

The next morning the three made their way to Francis's small hut. With their heads bowed, they were silent at first. One of them summoned enough courage to say: "Francis, may we stay with you? Will you teach us how to become Brothers, and be happy and satisfied as you are? Tell us, what should we do?"

Francis embraced each of them, gave them a brotherly kiss, and said: "Each one of you should build a small hut for yourself. There is much wonderful work waiting for you. Every day I will instruct you on how to become good Brothers." So, they all three stayed with Francis, and they even learned how to sing.

Clara and Her Sisters

In a castle in Assisi there lived a family of rich nobility. They had two daughters. The oldest, Clara, was especially beautiful. When she rode through the village people would turn to admire her countenance. One day Clara's nephew Rufino came for a visit to the castle. A short time earlier Francis had accepted him as one of his Brothers. Full of devotion, he told Clara about Francis's piety, his power of healing and his sermons. Clara listened. It happened that she was able to hear one of his sermons. His fiery words sunk deep into her soul. From that moment she thought about turning her life also to one of poverty and service.

Brother Rufino arranged for Francis and Clara to meet for a discussion. When Clara appeared with a trusted servant girl, Francis saw the possibility of forming a community of Sisters. Clara's heart leapt at the thought. In the coming Easter week she wanted to leave her castle home. Francis advised her to first enter a convent close to Assisi.

Palm Sunday arrived. Clara went to the cathedral mass for the last time as a lady of the nobility. She received a palm branch from the Bishop. The following night she left her parent's castle in the company of two friends. Since the night was brightened by an Easter full moon, they easily found their way to Portiuncula, where the Brothers were waiting for them. Carrying torches to light their way through the forest, Francis and Rufino met them. Soon all the Brothers were gathered in the small candle-lit church. There, by the altar, Clara took her leave from the outside world. She removed all her jewelry and left it to give to the poor. One Brother cut her hair short. Francis spoke about the duties of a Sisterhood. They could above all be useful in service to the sick and elderly and, in that way, share Christ's love with others.

At sunrise Francis and Rufino accompanied them to the small convent at Monte Subiaso. Later, a convent would be built at San Damiano.

On Easter evening Francis walked out with Brother Leo. He wondered: 'How will Sister Clara adjust to poverty?' The two men came upon a spring of water. Francis stared long into the water, without moving. When he finally looked up, he asked Brother Leo: "What do you think I saw in the water?"

Leo answered: "The Moon."

"No, I saw the face of our Sister Clara. It glowed with happiness and bliss. Christ has blessed her. Now I am certain she has found her way." So, with the help of Francis and his Brothers, Clara founded a convent at the little San Damiano Church.

The Fierce Wolf

Around the town of Gubbio, a wolf was on the prowl and it was spreading fear throughout the region. He not only devoured sheep and goats out of the herds, but he attacked people as well. The wolf would even leave some animals lying, torn to pieces in their own blood, without eating them. Whenever residents left the safety of the city walls, they would carry weapons. The fear of this wolf was very great, and nobody had been able to catch him up to now.

One day Francis was out hiking and he came to Gubbio. He heard the terrible story and decided to go meet the wolf. In spite of warnings from the townspeople, he went without so much as a stick. He was not far from the city gates when the wolf ran toward him and his companions with open jaws. Francis made a powerful sign of the Cross, and as the animal got closer, his gait slowed. The wolf closed his jaws, walked with his head lowered, and lay down on the ground at Francis's feet.

Francis began to speak to him. Later, the other Brothers told the people that Francis had addressed him as "Brother Wolf" and had scolded him about his horrible, bloodthirsty deeds. He also reproached the wolf for his disrespect of the townspeople.

During these accusations, the wolf gradually sank to the ground, his tail between his legs and his head bowed. While listening to Francis's words, his matted fur slowly became smooth again.

Francis said: "I will make peace between you and the people. They shall no longer pursue you, and their dogs will leave you alone.

The townspeople will put food out for you in front of their houses so you will not attack their sheep. Do you want this?"

The wolf was shaking as he stood up because Francis's forceful soul had taken command of him. He came very close to Francis and offered him his paw.

Many townspeople of Gubbio were watching from atop the city wall. A miracle was happening before their eyes! The news traveled quickly throughout the town, and all the townspeople gathered in front of the city gate.

Francis led the wolf through the gate and the folks gathered round. They could hardly believe what they were seeing. Some of them shrank back in fear, but Francis began to speak: "Listen, dear citizens of Gubbio! The wolf has promised to make peace with you, and to stop attacking your sheep and goats. In exchange, you must promise to leave food for him on your doorsteps. You may discuss among yourselves how this will be organized. From now on, no one from among you may harm the wolf. And he will not harm you. I will vouch for him. Dear citizens, will you agree to this?"

With a loud cry of approval, the gathered people agreed to feed the wolf.

So it happened, and even the village dogs stopped barking at Brother Wolf. This friendly peace lasted two years. When he came into the village during the day children would call out to him: "Caro Lupo! Dear wolf!" And they played with him; Francis had changed his soul.

The whole village mourned when the wolf died. Brother Wolf had served to keep Francis in their remembrance always – and the miraculous power of his great love.

The Cricket in the Fig Tree

A fig tree grew next to Francis's hut in Portiuncula. One summer morning Francis awoke to the chirping of a cricket. What a jubilee! He went outside to try to find the cricket musician. Francis discovered the cricket on a fig leaf. Francis liked to talk to animals, so he stuck out his hand and said: "Sister Cricket, come to me!" And what do you know? The little insect climbed onto his hand and began chirping again.

Francis wandered around the garden and conversed: "Let us praise the Creator for the beauty of the flowers! I will sing along with you." Francis sang with words about the beauty of the brilliant sunflowers, and he held the cricket up very close to the blooms. He sang of the rosebush and its aroma; he sang of the white lilies and the delicate grass. Brother Leo came out of his hut, stood still, and listened to the fine concert. After a while, he watched Francis carry the cricket back to the fig tree and set her on a leaf. The cricket stayed with them for a whole week.

Every day Francis went to the tree. The cricket would crawl upon his hand, and the walking, music-making and singing would begin anew. The other Brothers also watched and listened. Once, Leo tried to get the cricket to crawl onto his hand, but she hid in the leaves. Finally, Francis said to his little companion: "Now we will give our Sister Cricket leave!" She crawled out of sight and was never seen again.

The Bird Sermon

Francis was traveling with his group of Brothers, giving sermons to the people. As they approached the town of Bevagno, on both sides of the path countless birds were sitting and resting in the trees. A flock of birds had also landed in a nearby field. Francis said to his Brothers: "You rest here under the trees! I would like to give a sermon to the birds." The Brothers sat down in the shade and thought: 'With Francis, anything is possible.'

Francis went to the field, making strange, inviting sounds. Many of the birds flew to him; others sat in surrounding trees and bushes. Brother Leo was curious to see what would happen. Stealthily and unnoticed, he made his way closer to the field. He heard how Francis spoke in a lilting, sing-song voice: "Birds, dear Brothers and Sisters! The Creator has given you the sky and the air. You may fly freely wherever you wish. He gave you a feather coat to protect you from the cold. You neither sow nor harvest, but have everywhere food, and you drink from streams and rivers. You build your nests in the trees, forests and mountains. He gave you singing voices that sound like great songs of praise. You have listened well to me and, now, praise the Creator of the Universe!"

Just as Francis ended his speech, there arose loud singing and jubilation, but also some cawing, twittering and cackling. Many feathered and plumed creatures began beating their wings up and down. Brother Leo was amazed to see Francis raise his arms and make a large sign of the Cross toward the sky.

Suddenly the flocks of birds lifted off all at once. They flew away in the four directions of the cross: toward sunrise, sunset, the North and the South.

Whenever Francis came to a lake or river where there were fish, he would stick his hand in his pocket and take out some dry piece of bread, crumble it in his hands, and feed it to the fish. When they poked their heads above the water, he would say kind words to them. But nobody thought to write down those words, so there is no record of them.

Brother Donkey

Francis's mother had once told him: "The day before you were born, your father was away on a trip. An unknown, dignified, elderly gentleman came to me. He appeared to be on a pilgrimage. His speech was keen and serious. He swore to me that I would bring you into the world in a stable. As the time of your birth grew closer, I really did go with the nanny into the stable. The ox and donkey were standing there, and there was straw in the manger. When you were born, the nanny put you into the donkey's manger for a little while. That is probably why you have always had a great love for the donkey and always call him Brother Donkey."

During his travels, whenever Francis happened upon a farmer who had loaded his donkey with too many goods, and would even sit upon the donkey's back himself, Francis would stop him and say: "Are you not ashamed to have so many sacks upon your Brother Donkey's back, and then ride him yourself!? Please, get off the poor animal!" Then Francis would scratch the donkey's ears and pet his nose. Usually the farmer would dismount, and Francis would thank him.

Francis himself would always travel on foot. But later, when he was too weak or sick to walk, he was given a donkey. This animal loyally carried him from place to place so he could preach. No one was ever allowed to put the whip to his donkey. Instead, the animal was always guided by Francis's kind words.

The Grotto Christmas

One Christmas, Francis and his Brothers spent the special day in a grotto. It happened like this: Francis had a friend in Greccio who was respected and influential in the town. His name was Giovanni and he wanted to celebrate Christmas with Francis. Giovanni had told Francis about the grotto near the village. It was very like the one in Bethlehem that had served as shelter for the birth of Jesus. Francis said to Giovanni: "That is wonderful! For Christmas Eve, arrange to have some straw and a manger, and an ox and a donkey in the cave. I will come with my Brothers. We want to show the people in what poverty Jesus was born with a blessed, living picture. Our Priest, Silvestro, will say the Christmas Mass at the crèche."

This was two weeks before Christmas when Francis had that conversation with Giovanni. Men and women from Greccio donated candles and torches to light the grotto. When everything was arranged, Francis and his Brothers started toward the grotto just like the shepherds who went to Bethlehem; and behind them followed the townspeople. The forest echoed with singing. Everyone knelt in the cave. The Mass was begun. In a bright voice, Francis sang the Christmas Story from the Gospel of Luke. Then he preached a Christmas sermon to the gathered people: "Here, this manger is empty. But you can bring the Child forth in your heart and awaken it. *In dulci jubilo* – I rejoice in happiness!"

Unforgettable for everyone present, a second Bethlehem was celebrated there. From then on, churches have put up nativity scenes at Christmastime.

On Mount Alverno

During his travels, Francis would often preach day after day in order to comfort and strengthen the people because he felt compassion for them with their troubles and sorrows. But after a while, he started to feel a strong desire to withdraw and find a quiet place where he could be alone.

In Tuscany there lived a noble count by the name of Orlando. He had heard many wondrous things about Francis, but he had never had the opportunity to see or hear him in person. Now, Francis was traveling through Tuscany. One day, he climbed on top of a wall in a small village so he could preach from there. It happened that Count Orlando was visiting the same village that day. Full of expectation, he took his place amongt the listeners and was so happy that his wish to see and hear Francis was being fulfilled.

The wonderful sermon affected him deeply, to the core of his being. He went to Francis and said: "Honored Brother! I own a mountain in the Tuscan countryside. The area is quiet and secluded. It is called Alverno. This place would be well-suited for people like you who wish to live in holy seclusion. If you and your Brothers agree, I would be happy to make it a gift to you."

Francis replied: "I have long searched for just such a place. I will think about it, and I thank you for your generosity. When you have returned to your castle, I will send two Brothers to you so that they may visit the mountain and tell me about it."

So, a short time later, Francis sent two Brothers to the nobleman's castle. They were graciously received. Orlando sent a few servants to accompany them.to Mount Alverno. When they got to the top, they found a flat, open space – no house, no village, far and wide. Just as Orlando had instructed them, the servants built a few huts out of branches.

The two Brothers returned to Portiuncula with good news. In the summer, Francis chose three Brothers to accompany him to see Alverno for himself. Their names were Leo, Masseo and Angelo. The Brothers remaining behind blessed Francis. Their journey by foot lasted many days.

One evening they could not find a place to stay the night, neither a house nor a hostel. A thunderstorm was threatening. Finally, they came to a lonely, neglected pilgrim's chapel. Here they found protection and rest. The companions soon fell asleep, but Francis got up to pray. Out of cracks and niches wild, shadowy demons slipped out and beset the praying man. They yanked and tugged and harassed, trying to stop Francis from praying. But Francis remained firm and did not allow himself to be distracted. So the demons faded away.

In the morning the three Brothers noticed that Francis seemed weak, and his eye condition was flaring up. It had already caused him much pain in the past. It was difficult for him to continue walking. The Brothers were keeping a watchful eye for something that could help Francis. They saw a small farm. They asked the farmer: "We have a Brother with us who can hardly walk. Would you loan us a donkey?" As the farmer took in their brown robes, he asked: "Are you Brothers of Francis of Assisi, of whom I hear so much good?"

They replied: "Yes, he is with us. It is for him we wish to borrow a donkey." The farmer insisted on bringing the donkey to Francis himself. He carefully helped him mount the donkey.

When they were halfway to the top of Alverno, Francis stopped to rest in the shade of an oak tree. Some birds flew down, perched in the tree, and began to sing. Francis said to Angelo: "Do you hear? The mountain has sent the birds to welcome us."

When they got to the flat top, they found the huts built by the Count's servants completely undisturbed. They gave good shelter against the wind and weather. It was a quiet life of seclusion that the Brothers led.

Before Michaelmas, which is celebrated on the 29th of September, Francis wanted to spend forty days completely alone. The three Brothers built a small hermitage in the cliffs for Francis. Once a day, Brother Leo was allowed to bring him some bread and water. He would call out a greeting and the hermit would answer. In this solitude Francis was able to guide his soul consciously into the spiritual worlds, and angels visited him.

One day a quiet miracle occurred: In the early morning, when Brother Leo brought bread and wine and called out his greeting, there was no answer. He was worried. Hesitantly, he entered the hermitage. There he saw Brother Francis with his arms raised in prayer. As he looked more closely, a wonderful light, like a shimmering flame, suddenly appeared. It came down from the sky and surrounded the praying man. Brother Leo withdrew so he would not interrupt this divine occurrence.

From that time on, when Francis was with them again, the Brothers noticed the wounds of Christ, the crucified, were on

Francis's hands and feet. His right side looked as if it had been stabbed by a spear. Often, blood would flow out of this side wound. Francis hid from the people these signs of his encounter with Christ. The Brothers knew why, and they were worried that his life was slowly coming to an end.

As they were taking their leave from Mount Alverno in late autumn, Francis said: "This is the mountain of the angel!"

The Canticle of the Sun

During the summer before Francis's last summer on Earth, his eyes were almost blind from severe infection. He was to undertake a multiday trip, sitting on his donkey, to see a doctor. But after a few days, when they were nearing the convent of Sister Clara, Francis was overcome by weakness. He was carried into the convent gardens at San Damiano and a bed was made ready for him there. The summer nights were warm.

The next day Francis was still not better, so some helpful hands made a hut for him out of foliage and branches. Brothers Leo and Angelo took care of him. Sister Clara visited his bedside daily. Francis could no longer see the roses that were blooming in the garden, but their perfume wafted toward him. He could no longer observe the birds in the trees, but their singing brought joy to his soul. When Sister Clara sat with him, she would sing him songs and read to him from the Gospels.

Francis had not been in the hut very long before the garden mice realized that little crumbs were to be found there. Whenever Francis heard their rustling he would throw out a few nibbles for "Sister Mouse." So the number of mice continually grew and their activity became bolder. In the night, especially, they became a real plague. They scurried wildly and jumped around in the hut and did somersaults on the sick man's bed. While he would otherwise have been able to escape his pain through sleep, the mice kept him awake, and then he suffered from his infected eyes.

One night while he was tormented with pain, he remembered the appearance of Christ on Mount Alverno, where he had received the signs of His crucifixion wounds. A soft, golden radiance seemed to weave itself through his body. The pain disappeared. He was filled with the strength of the Sun. In spirit, he saw the illuminated Earth. The Sun, Moon and stars; the wind, clouds and springs; the animals and plants of the Earth and birds of the heavens – they were all his brothers and his sisters. He was filled indescribable joy: "I am, like all of you, born from God!"

Wonderful tones began to resound within him. Words sang in his soul. In the middle of the night Francis began to sing the "Canticle of the Sun." The singing eased his pain like a healing medicine. When Brother Leo arrived at the hut early the next morning, he heard joyful singing coming from inside. He went in and was amazed to hear the verses of the "Canticle of the Sun" that Francis had composed during the night. Angelo also came by, and they practiced the song together. Day after day, the three of them joyfully sang the Sun Song in praise of the Lord.

Il Cantico di Frate Sole

Altissimu, onnipotente, bon Signore,
Tue so le laude, la gloria, e l'honore et onne benedictione.
Ad Te solo, altissimo, se konfano,
Et nullu homo ène dignu Te mentouare.

Laudato sie, mi Signore, cum tucte le Tue creature,
Spetialmente messor lo frate Sole,
Lo qual è iorno; et allumini noi per lui.
Et ellu è bellu e radiante cum grande splendore:
De Te, Altissimo, porta significatione.

Laudato si, mi Signore, per sora Luna e le stelle:
In celu l'ài formate clarite, et pretiose et belle.

Laudato si, mi Signore, per frate Uento et per Aere,
Et nubilo et sereno et onne tempo,
Per lo quale, a le Tue creature dài sustentamento.

Laudato si, mi Signore, per sor' Aqua,
La quale è multo utile, et humile, et pretiosa et casta.

Laudato si, mi Signore, per frate Focu,
Per lo quale ennallumini la nocte:
Ed ello è bello e iucundo, e robustoso et forte.

Laudato si, mi Signore, per sora nostra Matre Terra,
La quale ne sustenta e gouerna,
Et produce diuersi fructi con coloriti fior et herba.

The Canticle of the Sun

Most high, all powerful, all good Lord!
All praise is Yours, all glory, all honor and all blessing.
To You, alone, Most High, do they belong.
No mortal lips are worthy to pronounce Your name.

Be praised, my Lord, through all Your creatures,
Especially through my lord Brother Sun,
Who brings the day; and You give light through him.
And he is beautiful and radiant in all his splendor:
Of, Most High, he bears the likeness.

Be praised, my Lord, through Sister Moon and the stars:
In the heavens You have made them bright, precious and beautiful.

Be praised, my Lord, through Brothers Wind and Air,
And clouds and storms, and all the weather,
Through which You give Your creatures sustenance.

Be praised, my Lord, through Sister Water;
She is very useful, and humble, and precious and pure.

Be praised, my Lord, through Brother Fire,
Through whom You brighten the night:
He is beautiful and cheerful, and powerful and strong.

Be praised, my Lord, through our Sister Mother Earth,
Who feeds us and rules us,
And produces various fruits with colored flowers and herbs.

The Peacemaker

The last summer faded away. The year was nodding toward autumn. The Bishop of Assisi wanted to provide care for Francis at his palace. So, Francis was taken to the large, stone house in the city. Brother Leo and Brother Angelo continued to care for the now very sick man.

It came to Francis's attention that the Bishop and the Mayor of Assisi were in a dispute and had become enemies – over worldly matters. Concerned, he asked: "Is there no one who will try to make peace between these two important men?" But nobody volunteered. So Francis composed a new verse for the Sun Song, a verse about forgiveness:

> *Laudato si, mi Signore, per quelli*
> *Ke perdonano per lo Tuo amore*
> *Et sustengono infirmitate et tribulantione.*
> *Beati quelli ke 'l sosterrano in pace,*
> *Ka da Te, Altissimo, siranno incoronati.*

> Be praised, my Lord, through those
> Who forgive for love of you;
> Through those who endure sickness and trial.
> Happy are those who endure in peace,
> For by you, Most High, they will be crowned.

Now, Francis asked two of his Brothers: "Go to the Mayor and bring him my greetings. Ask him in my name to come here to the palace. I have something important to tell him."

The Mayor admired Francis greatly, and so he answered the call. He also brought a few city councilmen with him. When they arrived in the courtyard of the palace, at Francis's bidding, the Bishop also appeared.

Francis had asked two Brothers to sing the Sun Song to those gathered and include the new verses. Before they began singing, one of Francis's messengers said: "This song of praise we are about to sing – Francis has requested that you take it into your hearts and think about it!" The Mayor stood and folded his hands.

The Brothers began to sing, verse after verse. Through an open window, the song drifted up to Francis in his sick bed and permeated his prayer for peace. Then the last verse was sung:

> Be praised, my Lord, through those
> Who forgive for love of you;
> Through those who endure sickness and trial.
> Happy are those who endure in peace,
> For by you, Most High, they will be crowned.

Both the Bishop and the Mayor were deeply moved. The Mayor went to the Bishop and offered him his hand in forgiveness. They gave each other a heartfelt embrace as witnessed by all present. The plan of forgiveness had worked.

The Brothers and all others there were amazed and happy. They saw it as a miracle that Francis had brought peace again to the city of Assisi.

Farewell to Earthly Life

The Brothers knew that Francis did not feel comfortable in the rich surroundings of the palace – him, the bridegroom of poverty, even though his blindness kept him from seeing the grandeur of the marble rooms.

When the sick man felt that he must soon die, he asked to be taken back to Portiuncula. He wanted to end where he had begun. He was carried on a stretcher down to the valley. Halfway there, Francis asked that the stretcher be lowered. He sat up a little and spoke a blessing in the direction of the city: It should remain a dwelling place of peace and the Christian Spirit!

During the few days he remained alive, he often asked his Brothers: "Sing me the Sun Song!" He directed that a loaf of bread be broken into small pieces and placed upon a platter. He gave each Brother present a piece of the bread with his blessing. Afterward, he composed one last verse for the Sun Song, dedicated to Brother Death:

> *Laudato si, mi Signore, per sora nostra Morte corporale,*
> *Da la quale nullu homo uiuente pò skappare.*
> *Guai a quelli ke morrano ne le peccata mortali.*
> *Beati quelli ke trouerà ne le Tue sanctissime uoluntati,*
> *Ka la morte secunda no 'l farrá male.*
> *Laudate e benedicete mi Signore*
> *Et rengratiate e seruiteli cum grande humilitate.*

Be praised, my Lord, through our Brother Bodily Death,
From whose embrace no living person can escape.
Woe to those who die in mortal sin.
Happy those he finds doing Your most holy will,
The second death can do no harm to them.
Praise and bless my Lord and give thanks,
And serve him with great humility.

On the evening of his death a flock of larks surrounded the thatch roof under which Francis lay. And the birds sang late into the night as his soul entered the path to Heaven.

Other books by Jakob Streit
Translated from the German by Nina Kuettel

This powerful story tells of the life of Columban, his travels from Ireland, his many adventures, his life in the Inner Hebrides on the island of Iona in Scotland and beyond. It is a story that makes the Middle Ages come alive and can be a valuable class reader. ISBN 978-1-936367-01-9

The story of St. Odelia, patron saint in the Alsace region of France, is one of the most beautiful legends known from the Middle Ages. It is about the destiny of a child, born blind and turned out by her father, who gains her sight through a miracle at her baptism. The young girl goes her way, unerringly and against all odds, and establishes the convent later names for her: Odelienberg. ISBN 978-1-936367-05-4

Invisible Guardians is a collection of stories of first-hand experiences of intervention before a death event. They are inspiring and can be used together as a reader or as individual stories read to children.
ISBN 978-1-936367-17-7

The Star Rider is a free adaptation of a legend told by the elderly O'Daly. The legend is believed to have emerged in the 17th century. *Anna McLoon* is a story from modern times. Together with a friend, the author went in search of the last Celtic storyteller, who had spent a lifetime going from farm to farm, village to village throughout all of Ireland, telling her treasure of Irish folktales. The illustrations are reproductions of copper etchings by Andrez Dauchez from a publication by the Societé des amis du livre moderne, *Le Foyer Breton* by Emile Souvestre. ISBN 978-1-888365-95-5

What Animals Say to Each Other is a collection of 30 nature fables told in rhyme. When two so very different animals such as a squirrel and a toad start talking, we can enjoy the poetry of their conversation as well as the humor. Beautifully illustrated with B&W drawings by a 13-year-old student.
ISBN 978-1-938367-23-8

Also available from AWSNA Publications

 Jakob Streit was born in 1910 in the picturesque village of Spiez on the Lake of Thun in Switzerland. He lived there for almost 99 years, until his death in 2009. His father was a watchmaker, and his mother had a talent for languages. He grew up with his five siblings, helping to care for his father's many bee hives, as well as the cow and some sheep.

The teacher's college in Bern led to his first career as an elementary grades school teacher until his retirement. He employed the Waldorf teaching method as much as possible in his public school classroom. His early children's books evolved out of the stories he would tell his students, especially the nature stories. Between 1940 and 2004 he wrote over forty children's books that encompass a variety of themes: the beloved nature stories, Bible stories retold, biographies and historical fiction, to name a few.

He was also an accomplished pianist and organist. His interest in the performing arts led to his being chosen as the director of the Swiss National Theater in Interlaken where a play about William Tell was performed annually at an outdoor theater. He acted as director from 1947 to 1952. He also directed several operas at the Castle Theater in Spiez including *The Magic Flute* and *Orpheus*.

Jakob Streit concerned himself with questions of art and art history his entire life. His knowledge of anthroposophy and Waldorf education led to a second career as a sought-after lecturer in Central Europe for many years after his retirement from teaching. He also wrote many more books in his later years, including seven works of non-fiction.